Coloring Books For Adults
Volume 19

Stained Glass Windows 3

50 Mind Calming And Stress Relieving Patterns

Audrey Wingate

Copyright © 2016 Audrey Wingate

All rights reserved.

No part of this book may be reproduced by any means whatsoever without the written permission of the author.

ISBN: 978-1-5391-5540-9

The True Joy Of Coloring

Many adults and older children today are reconnecting with their inner childhood and returning to coloring for both relaxation and to unlock their creativity.

Coloring is a form of active meditation and focusing your attention on the simple and repetitive tasks of bringing a black and white outline to life in beautiful and vibrant color drives away the negative thoughts and clutter of daily living, calming the mind and bringing peace to your life.

For older individuals, coloring is also extremely useful in helping to calm and center the mind, maintain the essential focusing ability of the brain and exercise those all important fine motor skills.

And don't forget that coloring is not only extremely helpful when practiced individually, but is also a great and growing family activity.

So, find a quiet corner, get out those colors and enjoy!

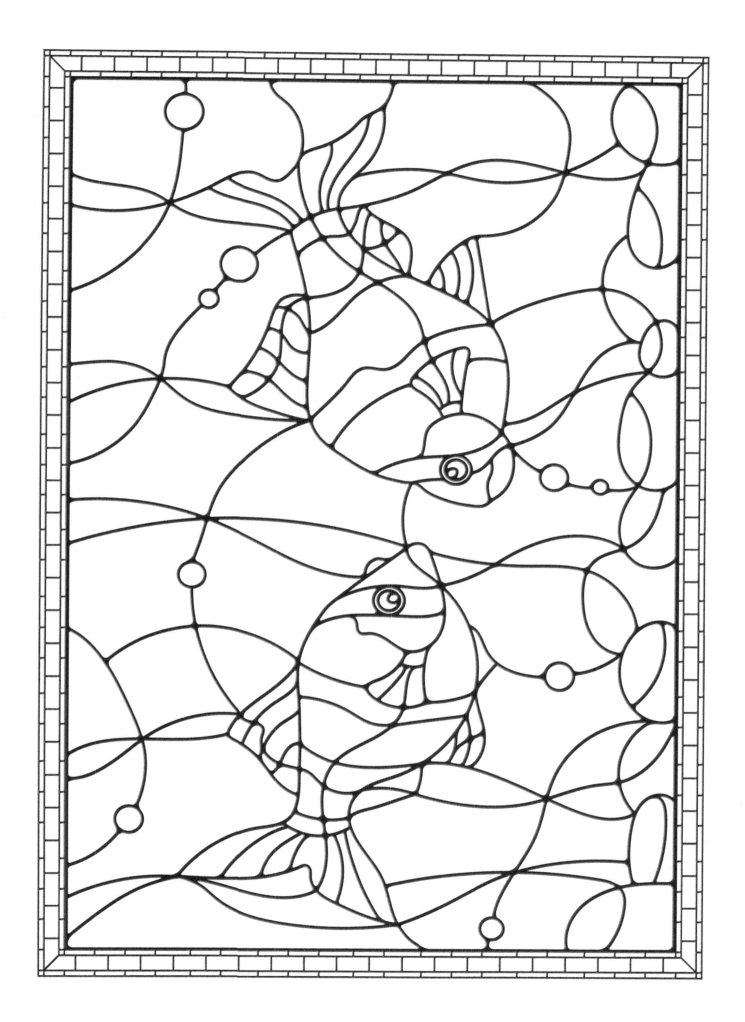

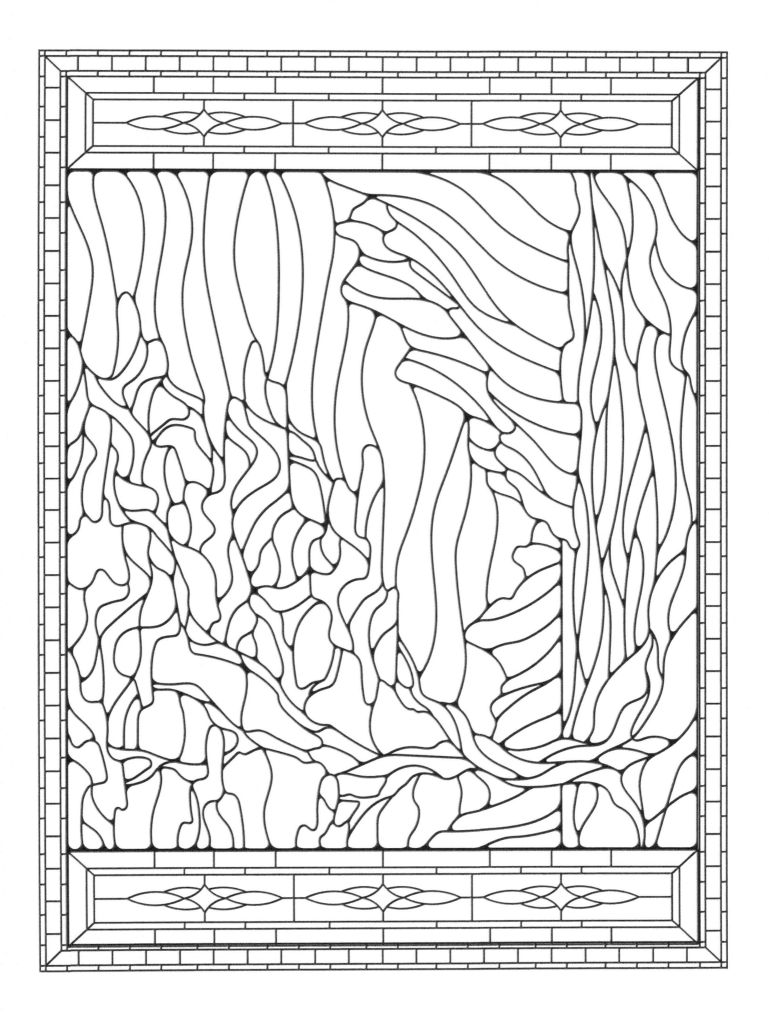

For other coloring books by Audrey Wingate please visit:

http://WMCPublishing.com/Audrey-Wingate

Made in the USA
Middletown, DE
25 August 2019